WHY DID HITLER HATE JEWS?

History Book War
Children's Holocaust Books

Speedy Publishing LLC

40 E. Main St. #1156

Newark, DE 19711

www.speedypublishing.com

Copyright 2017

In this book, we're going to talk about why Adolf Hitler hated the Jewish people. So, to begin, let's review the history before World War II.

WHAT IS ANTI-SEMITISM?

Anti-Semitism means hostility or prejudice toward Jewish people. Before Adolf Hitler rose to power in Germany, there was already anti-Semitism in Europe. The term "anti-Semitism" dates back to the 1870s, however, even in ancient times there was a great deal of hostility toward the Jewish people. They were banished from their homeland many times by governments such as the Roman Empire, which destroyed their Second Temple in 70 AD, forty years after the death of Christ.

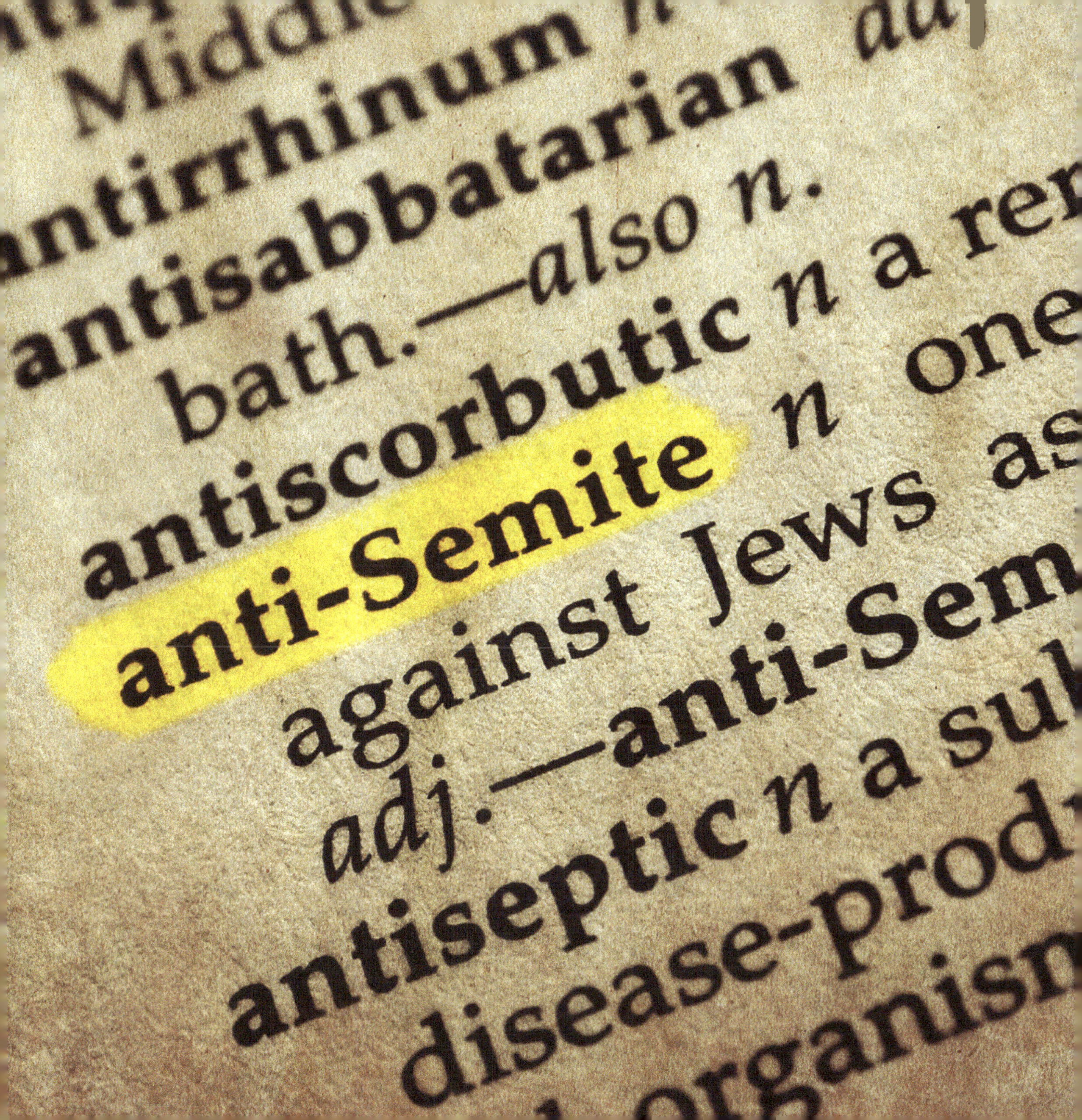
Middle
antirrhinum n
antisabbatarian ad
bath.—also n.
antiscorbutic n a re
anti-Semite n one
against Jews as
adj.—anti-Sem
antiseptic n a su
disease-prod
organism

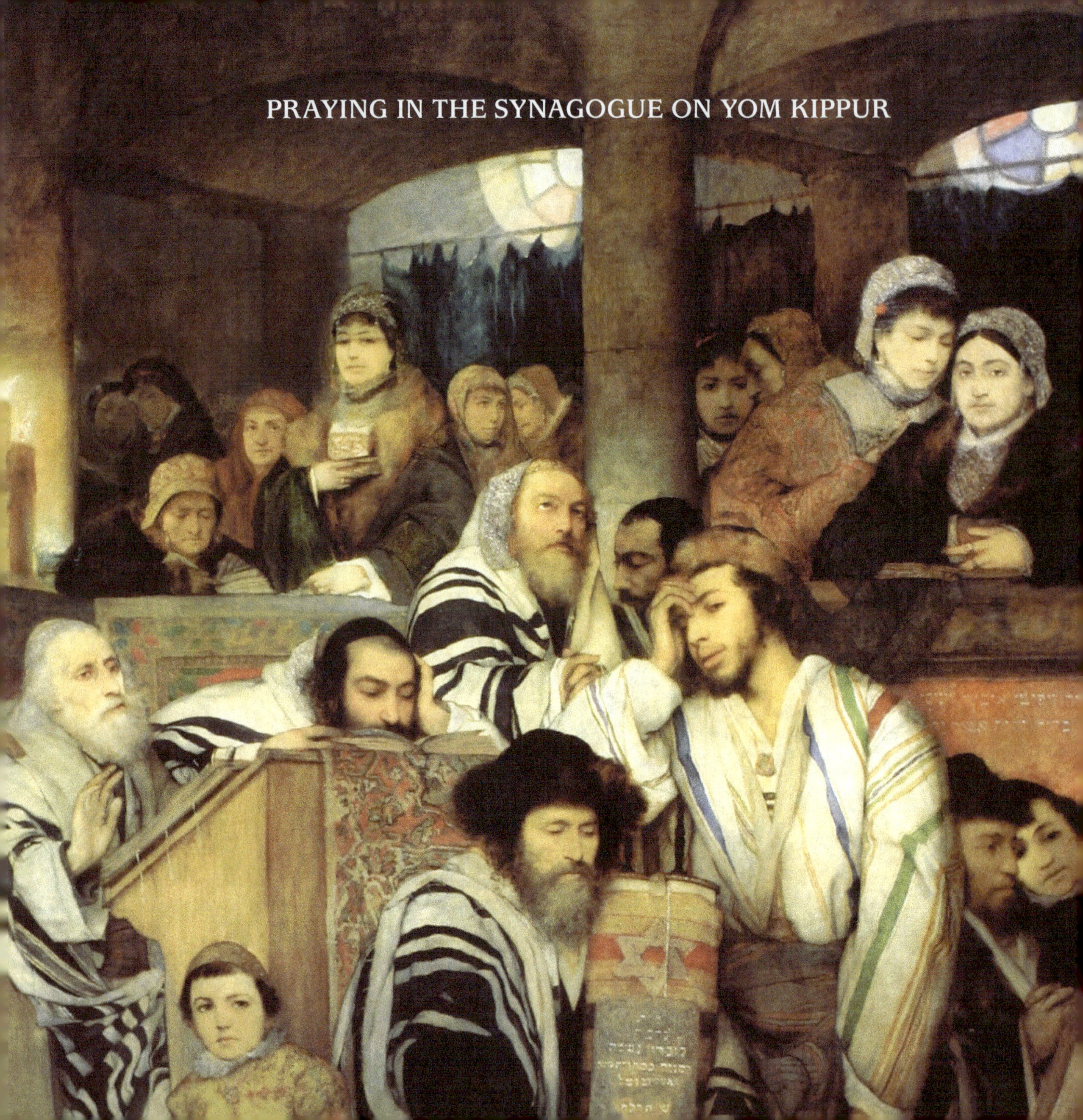

When the Age of Enlightenment began in the 17th century, there was a movement toward tolerance of many different types of religions. When Napoleon was in power in the 19th century, he approved laws that ended restrictions that had been placed on the Jews. However, many people in Europe still disliked Jewish people. Their hatred seemed to be based more upon racial prejudice than religious intolerance.

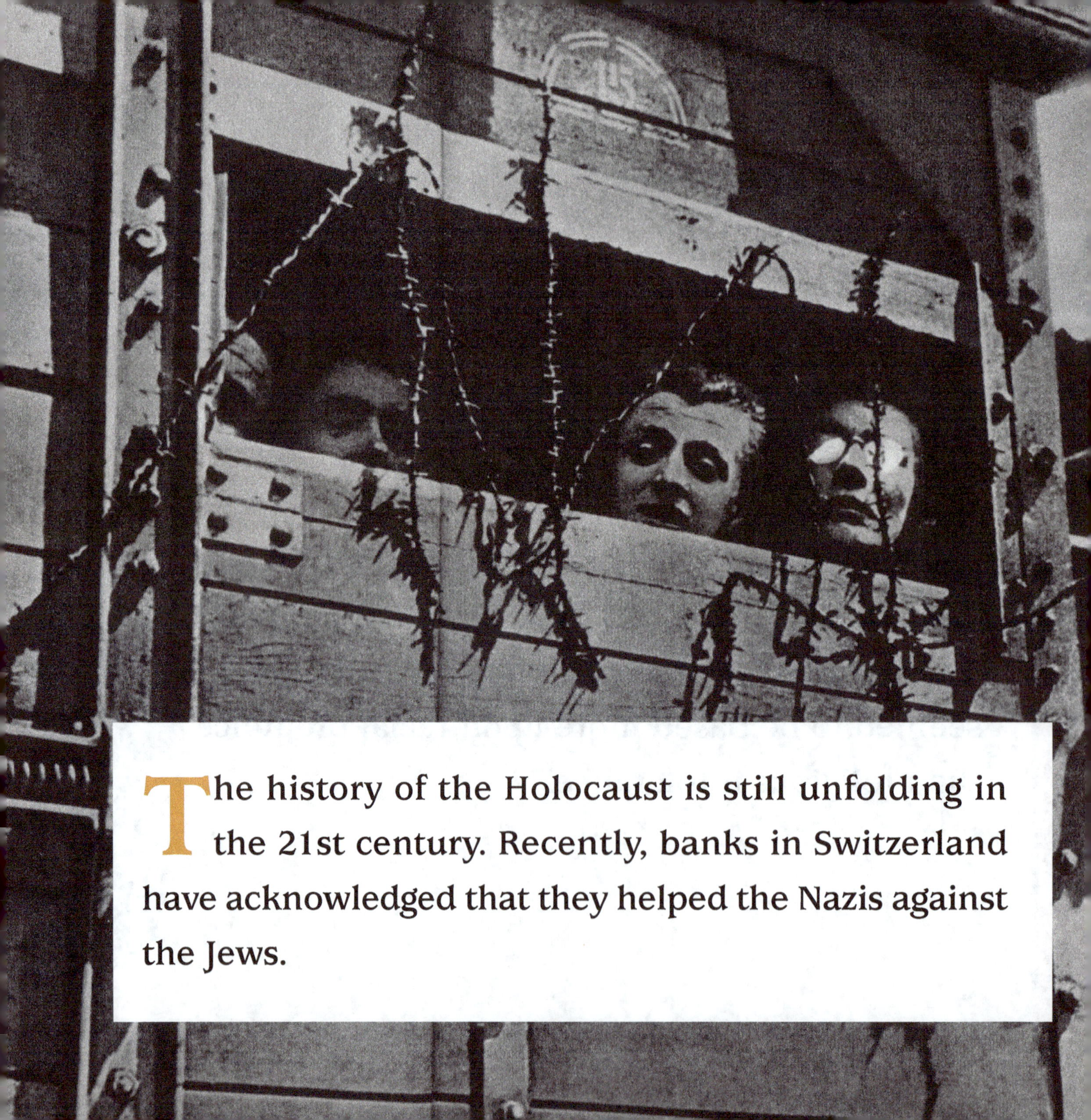

The history of the Holocaust is still unfolding in the 21st century. Recently, banks in Switzerland have acknowledged that they helped the Nazis against the Jews.

They are trying to make up for their misdeeds by establishing financial funds for survivors of the Holocaust and their children, but no amount of money could ever repay the Jewish people for what they have endured.

ADOLF HITLER

WHY DID HITLER HATE THE JEWISH PEOPLE?

dolf Hitler was born in Austria in 1889. As an adult, he was a soldier in the German army during the first World War. This was the beginning of his hatred for the Jews. At that time, there were many anti-Semites in the country of Germany. They thought the Jewish people were responsible for their country's defeat during World War I in 1918.

Hitler thought that Jewish people were less than human. He believed that the "pure race" of Germans, who were called the Aryan race, were superior to other human beings. He intended to use the principles of evolution and Darwinism to develop a race of perfect human beings based on the Aryan race.

JEWISH REFUGEES AT CROYDON AIRPORT 1939

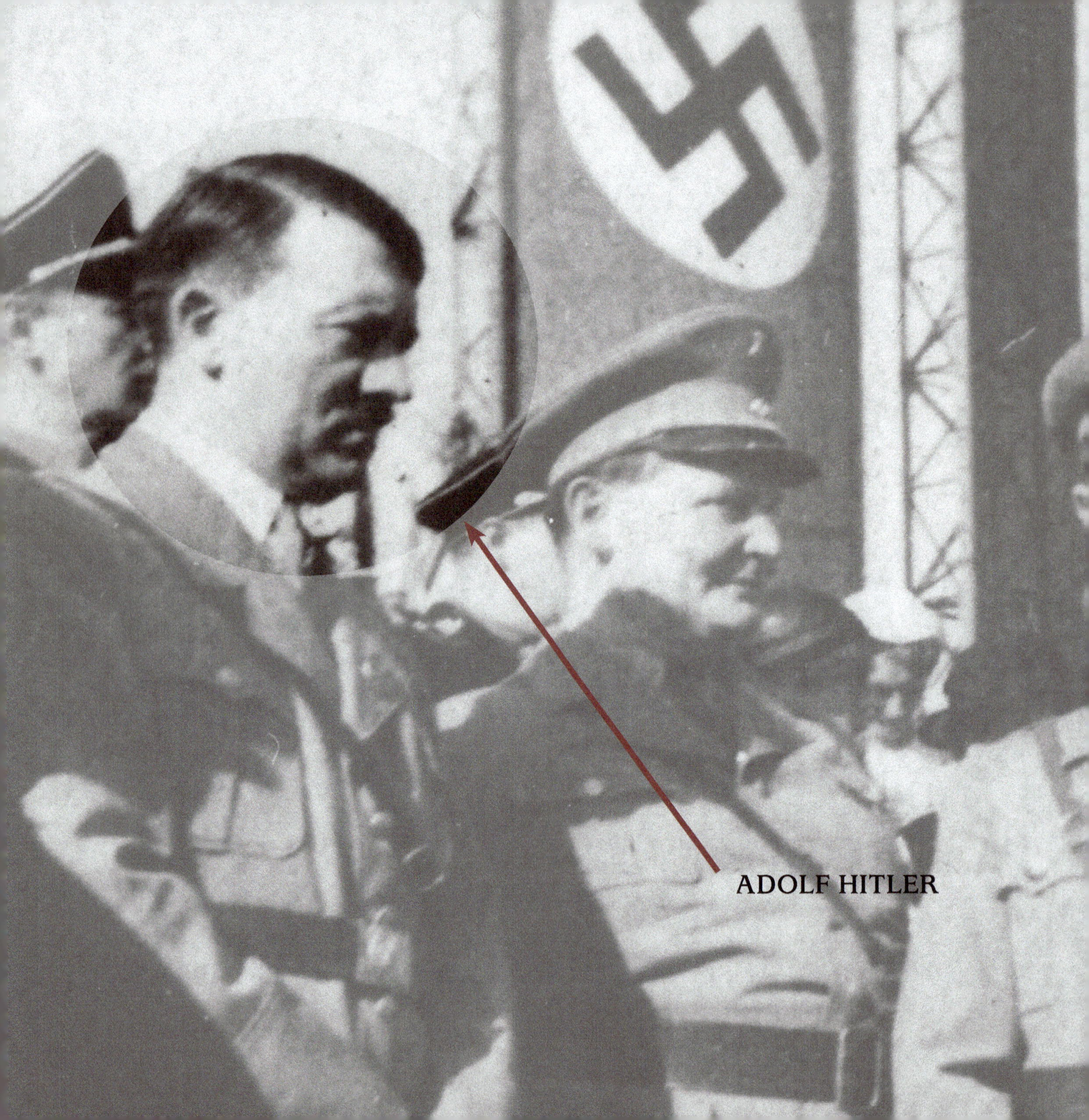

ADOLF HITLER

After the first World War was over, Hitler became a member of the National German Workers Party. Eventually, this political group was known as the Nazis.

itler and his group tried to take over Bavaria, a section of Germany, in the incident called the Beer Hall Putsch in 1923. The attempt failed and Hitler was thrown into prison. While in prison, he wrote the now-famous book "Mein Kampf," which means "My Struggle." He made a prediction that there would be a war in Europe soon and that this war would mean "the end of the Jewish people living in Germany."

Adolf Hitler

Mein Kampf
Von
Adolf Hitler
Zwei Bände in einem Band
Ungekürzte Ausgabe

Erster Band:
Eine Abrechnung

Zweiter Band:
Die nationalsozialistische Bewegung

534.–537. Auflage

1940

Zentralverlag der NSDAP., Frz. Eher Nachf., GmbH.,
München

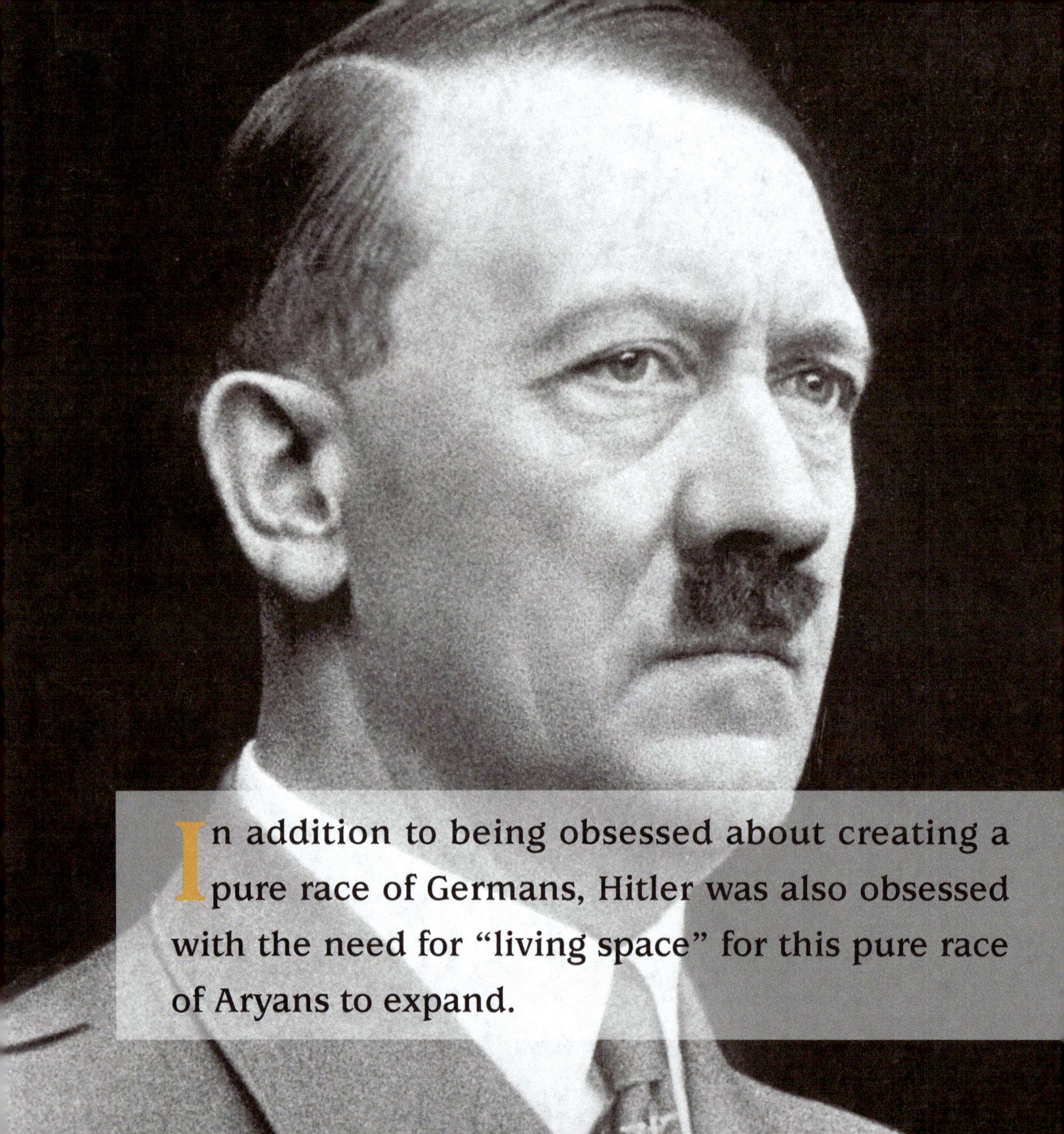
In addition to being obsessed about creating a pure race of Germans, Hitler was also obsessed with the need for "living space" for this pure race of Aryans to expand.

This need was called "Lebensraum" and it explains why Hitler began to take over surrounding countries once he came into power.

Ten years after he was released from prison, he was able to outmaneuver his rivals and put his party and himself in a position of power. In January of 1933, he became Germany's chancellor. After the President of Germany, Paul von Hindenburg, died in 1934, Hitler named himself the supreme ruler of the country. He was the "Fuhrer."

THE NAZI REVOLUTION

From 1933 to 1939, Hitler went forward with his evil plans. Everything he did revolved around the need for "racial purity" for the Germans and expansion so that their Aryan race could dominate the Earth.

At the beginning, they began by persecuting Communists as well as Social Democrats. Their first concentration camp was located at Dachau, near Munich, and many of the prisoners that were shipped there had Communist affiliations.

DACHAU CONCENTRATION CAMP

HEINRICH HIMMLER

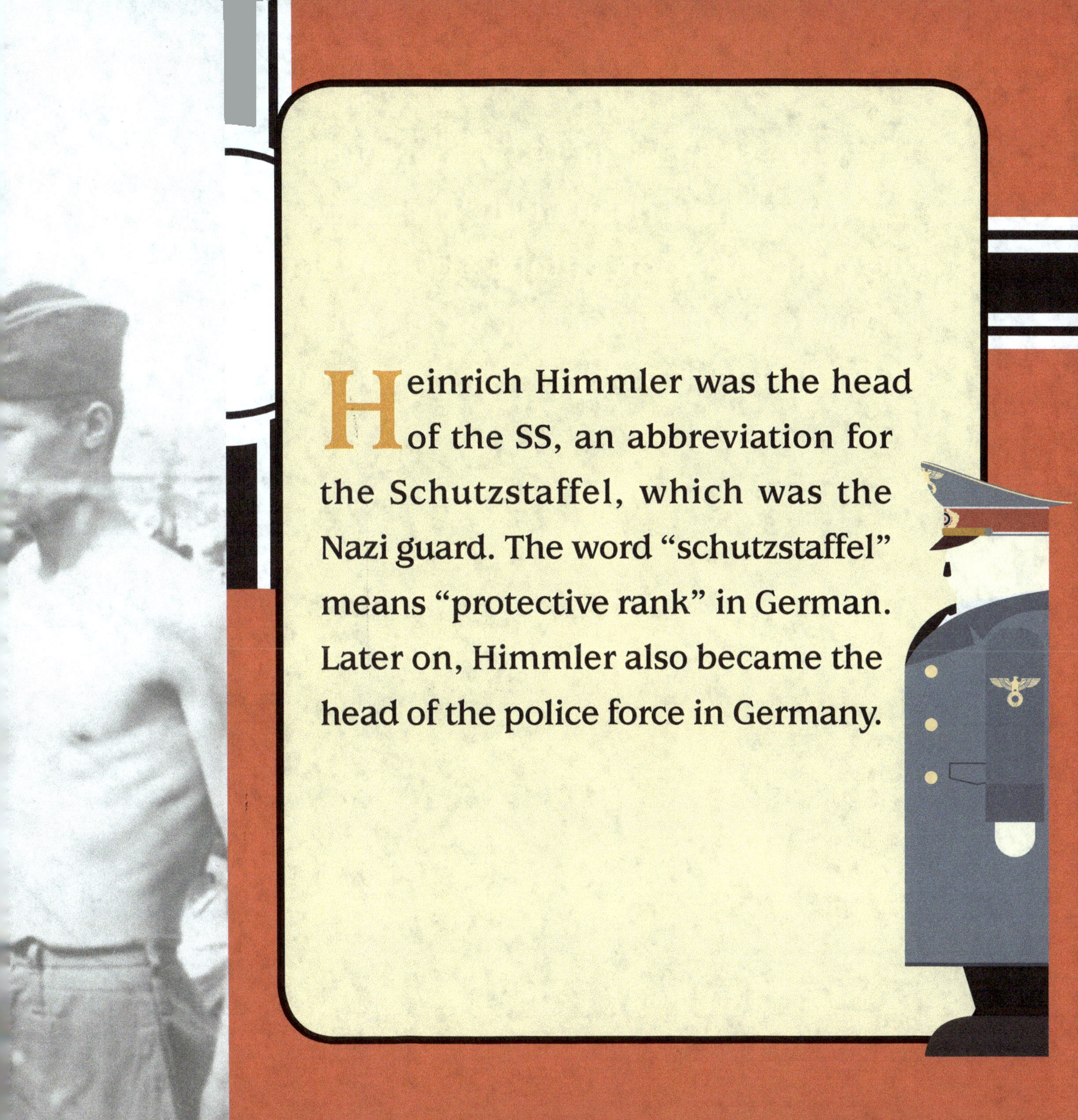

Heinrich Himmler was the head of the SS, an abbreviation for the Schutzstaffel, which was the Nazi guard. The word "schutzstaffel" means "protective rank" in German. Later on, Himmler also became the head of the police force in Germany.

By the summer of 1933, there were over 25,000 people imprisoned in "protective custody" in the concentration camps of Germany. The Nazis began to burn books that were written by Jews or Communists in a show of their strength.

BOOKS WERE BURNED BY NAZIS

JEWS GOING TO CONCENTRATION CAMP

At that time, the number of Jewish people living in Germany was about 525,000. From 1933 through 1939, the Germans began to purge the non-Aryans from all civil service jobs. They took clients away from lawyers and doctors of Jewish descent and began to liquidate businesses that were owned by Jewish people.

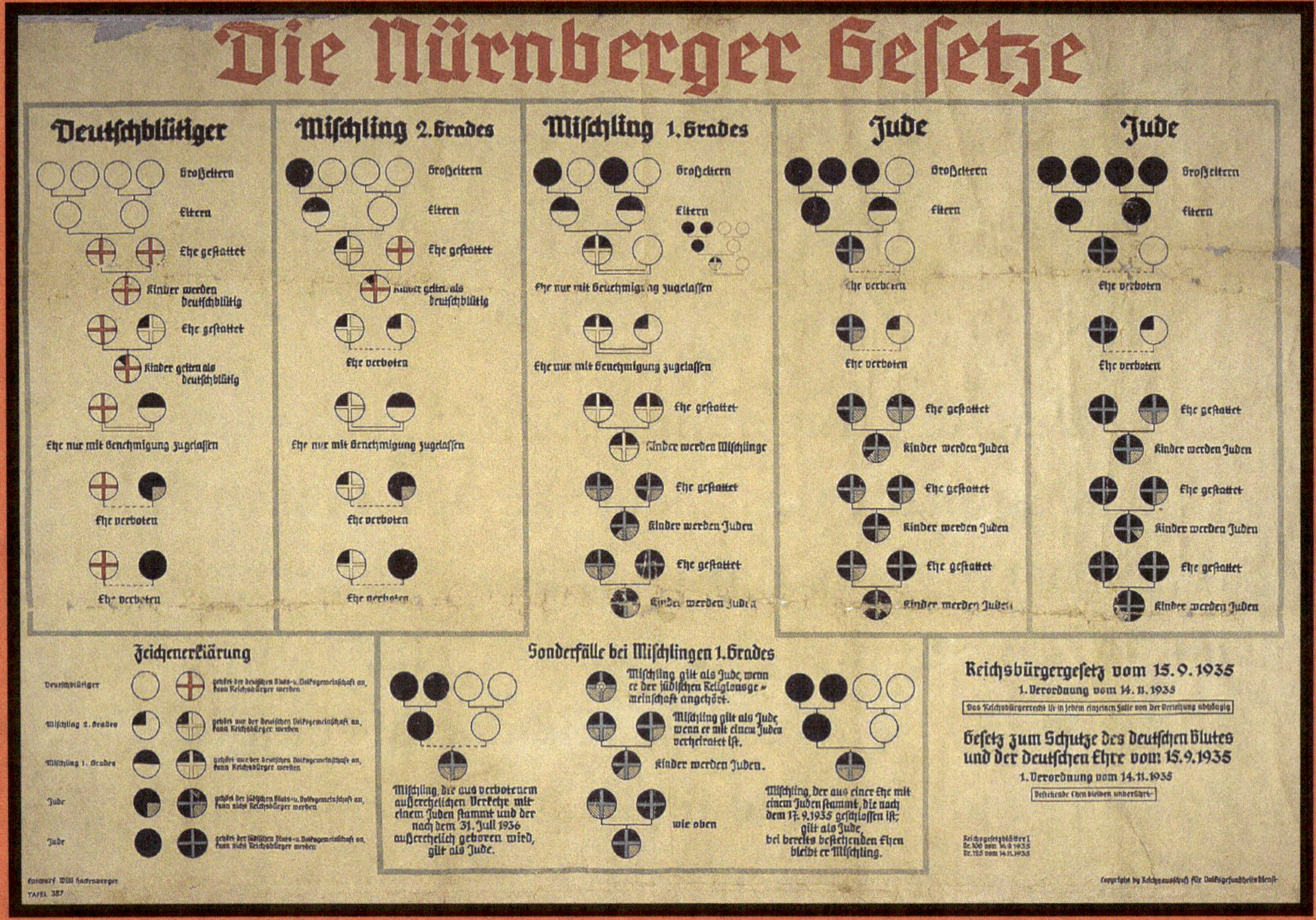

U nder laws the Nazis had passed in 1935, called the Nuremberg Laws, people who had 3 or 4 grandparents with Jewish heritage were called half-breeds.

They became targets of persecution. This conflict erupted in Kristallnacht, which translates to "the night of broken glass," which occurred in 1938.

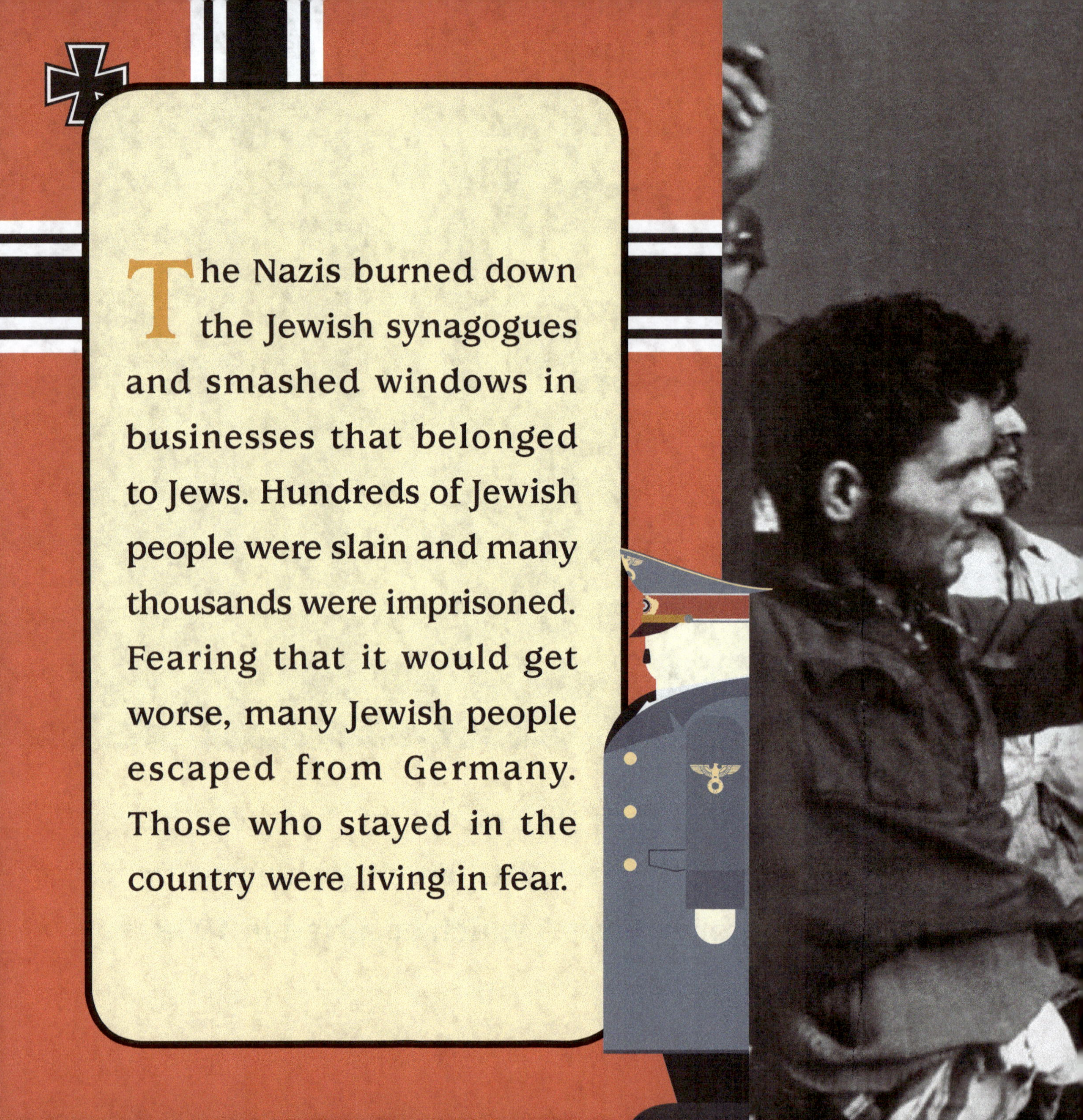

The Nazis burned down the Jewish synagogues and smashed windows in businesses that belonged to Jews. Hundreds of Jewish people were slain and many thousands were imprisoned. Fearing that it would get worse, many Jewish people escaped from Germany. Those who stayed in the country were living in fear.

JEWS WERE CAPTURED

SYNAGOGUE AT NUREMBERG

THE BEGINNING OF WORLD WAR II, 1939 TO 1940

In the fall of 1939, the Nazis began to occupy Poland and the German SS forced thousands of Jewish people to leave their homes and become prisoners in ghettoes. The Polish Jews had to give their lands and homes to non-Jews in Poland who identified themselves as Germans or Germans from the Nazi Reich.

The ghettoes were surrounded by tall walls and fences of barbed wire. They functioned as if they were prisoner city-states even though they were governed by councils of Jews.

There was intense poverty and hunger in these ghettoes and they were breeding grounds for serious diseases like typhus.

GAS CHAMBER AT AUSCHWITZ

Another part of Hitler's plan was to get rid of people who had genetic defects. Beginning in 1939, over 70,000 people with physical and mental disabilities were gassed to death in Hitler's Euthansia Program. When some of the religious leaders in Germany found out, they protested, and Hitler ended this program in 1941.

JEWISH WOMEN AND CHILDREN SELECTED FOR
DEATH WALK TOWARD THE GAS CHAMBER

This program was like a test for Hitler's "Final Solution," which would come next.

Hitler's soldiers marched in and conquered many of the countries of Europe to expand the Nazi Empire. Starting in 1941, Jewish people from all over the continent in addition to thousands of gypsies were shipped to the ghettoes of Poland.

JEWS GOING TO POLAND

BATTLE OF MOSCOW

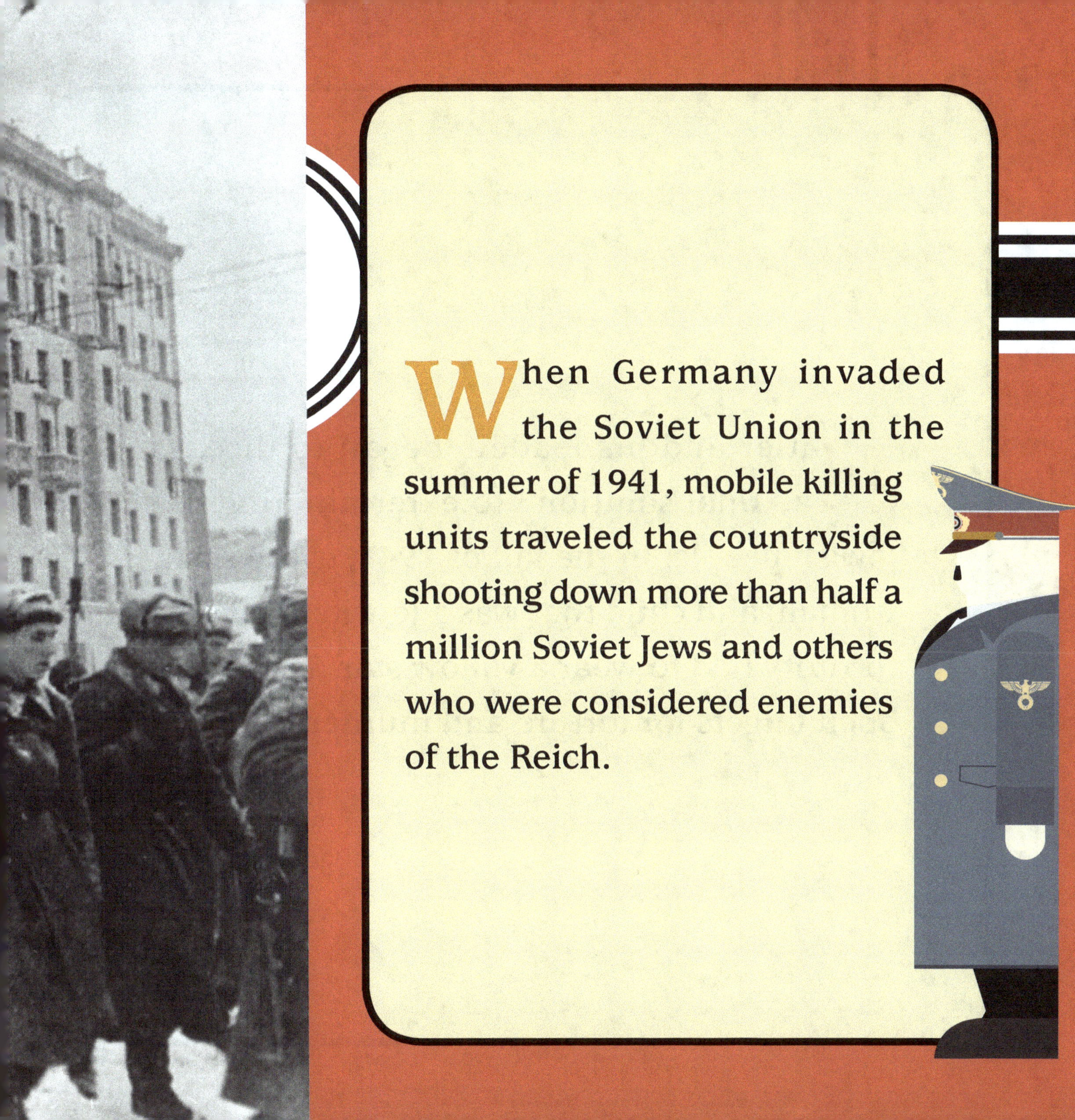

When Germany invaded the Soviet Union in the summer of 1941, mobile killing units traveled the countryside shooting down more than half a million Soviet Jews and others who were considered enemies of the Reich.

Hitler and his leaders began to discuss a "final solution" to exterminating the Jewish people. In the fall of 1941, every man, woman, and child that was a Jew in a German territory had to wear a yellow star. They were open targets for torture and murder.

Thousands were shipped to the ghettoes in Poland as well as to the cities in the Soviet Union where the Germans had control. The Nazis had been experimenting with killing huge numbers of people at the Auschwitz concentration

camp located near Krakow, Poland. They had used a pesticide to kill 500 prisoners of war from the Soviet Union. They placed a huge order for more pesticide to begin the Holocaust.

THE HOLOCAUST DEATH CAMPS, 1941 TO 1945

At the end of 1941, the Nazis began to organize mass transportation of Jewish people from Poland's ghettoes to the concentration camps. They began with those they felt could not help them with manual labor. The first gassings started at Belzec in 1942. Other centers for mass killing were set up at camps that had been built in the occupied sections of Poland.

MASS TRANSPORTATION TO
CONCENTRATION CAMPS

AUSCHWITZ-BIRKENAU

There were five major camps that were designed for extermination: Chelmno, Treblinka, Sobibor, Majdanek, and the largest and perhaps the most dreaded of all, Auschwitz-Birkenau.

The Nazis attempted to keep their crimes secret, but the killings were so massive that it was impossible. Eyewitnesses risked their lives to ensure that the Allied Powers found out what was happening. However, for quite some time the Allied leaders didn't believe that such a large number of people could be murdered.

At the Auschwitz camp alone, over 2 million people were exterminated by gas and their bodies were burned for disposal in giant crematoriums. Thousands more died of disease or from starvation.

MASS GRAVE AT BERGEN-BELSEN
CONCENTRATION CAMP

THE STARS AND STRIPES

GERMANY EDITION
Volume 1, No. 35
Wednesday, May 2, 1945

Daily Newspaper of U.S. Armed Forces — in the European Theater of Operations

KAPUTT

HITLER DEAD

Adolf Hitler, for 12 years the master of Germany and the man who set out to conquer the world, died yesterday afternoon, the German radio at Hamburg announced last night. Declaring that Grand Admiral Karl Doenitz, commander-in-chief of the German Navy, was

7th Clears Munich

Yank Armor Across Elbe

Munich, capital of Bavaria and home of the Nazi movement, today was completely in the hands of 7th Army troops.

Far to the north, troops of the U.S. 2d Armored Div. linked up with British units under Field Marshal Bernard L. Montgomery's command

Reds Gain on Baltic, Race Into Moravia

MOSCOW, May 1 (Reuter)—Capture of Stralsund, on the Baltic Sea opposite the island naval base of Ruegen, was announced tonight in an order of the day from Marshal Stalin.

Marshal Rokossovsky's 2d White Russian Army had also advanced to within 30 miles of Rostock, and Genmin, Msichin, Waren and Wesenberg important communications centers, have fallen.

On the southern front, the Soviet offensive in Czechoslovakia

Hitler's successor, the radio stated:

"It is reported from Der Fuehrer's headquarters that Der Fuehrer, Adolf Hitler, has fallen this afternoon at his command post in the Reich Chancellery, fighting to the last breath against Bolshevism and for Germany."

Death Is Not Explained

The announcement did not explain how Hitler, who was 56 years old 12 days ago, had "fallen." Russian forces in recent

streets with white flags.

Against this, however, some 55 battalions had made suicide pacts to go down with the battle

By 1945, it was clear that Hitler and the Nazis were losing the war. In his bunker in Germany, Hitler wrote out his will and his final political statement. In that document, he blamed the outbreak of the war on the Jewish people and urged the people of Germany to continue with the "observance of racial laws." On April 30, 1945, he took his own life. After the war was over, the crimes of the Nazi Reich were exposed and the people of the world were horrified at what had happened during the Holocaust.

SUMMARY

itler hated the Jewish people and considered them to be less than human. The Nazis felt that their race, the Aryan race, was superior to other races. They wanted to expand their race and exterminate the Jews. Hitler and the other members of the Nazi party killed over 6 million Jews during World War II. This horrible tragedy is called the Holocaust.

Now that you know more about the background of the Holocaust you may want to find out more information about the country of Israel in the Baby Professor book Why Was Israel Called the Holy Land – History Book for Kids.

Visit

www.BabyProfessorBooks.com

to download Free Baby Professor eBooks
and view our catalog of new and exciting
Children's Books